Resources for Observation and Reflection

Janet Gonzalez-Mena
Napa Valley College

Boston   Burr Ridge, IL   Dubuque, IA   Madison, WI   New York   San Francisco   St. Louis
Bangkok   Bogot   Caracas   Lisbon   London   Madrid   Mexico City
Milan   Montreal   New Delhi   Santiago   Seoul   Singapore   Sydney   Taipei   Toronto

The McGraw·Hill Companies

Resources for Observation and Reflection
to accompany
Foundations of Early Childhood Education: Teaching Children in a Diverse Society
Janet Gonzalez-Mena

Published by McGraw-Hill, an imprint of The McGraw-Hill Companies, Inc.,
1221 Avenue of the Americas, New York, NY 10020. Copyright 2005 by
The McGraw-Hill Companies, Inc. All rights reserved.

1 2 3 4 5 6 7 8 9 0 QPD/QPD 9 0 9 8 7 6 5 4

ISBN 0-07-287786-3

www.mhhe.com

Contents

Resources for Observation and Reflection

Introduction

This workbook accompanies *Foundations of Early Childhood Education: Teaching Children in a Diverse Society*, 3rd edition. It will facilitate your studies of the care and education of young children. The first section is an observation guide, which gives guidelines, instructions, and chapter-by-chapter activities for using observation to learn about young children, their development, and learning in educational settings through using various observation strategies. The second section helps you review and think about information in the chapters. It is based on the idea that writing thoughts down helps clarify and expand them. These questions are different from the reflection questions in the text itself. Those are designed to help you look inside yourself at your experiences and personal issues and the feelings attached. The reflection questions here help you think back about what you learned in reading the chapter and then go deeper into the subject matter by expanding on it, analyzing and/or figuring out ways to apply it. The third section contains a listing of resources including journals, books, and videos that can expand your knowledge of early care and education. Finally, the last section contains the NAEYC Accreditation Standards plus four NAEYC position statements to which the text refers.

—Janet Gonzalez-Mena

Observation Guide

Introduction to Observation

Why Observe?

Observation is an important part of any teacher's job and is ongoing. The younger the child or the fewer communication skills the child has, the more important it is to continually observe. How else are you to know what each child needs minute to minute, plus how to respond to and interact with the child? Through observation you can change the mode of interaction to fit. You also learn from observing over time about the child's temperament and what makes this child unique. As you discover how best to communicate and how to read the child's various modes of communication, you build and solidify your relationship with that child. Though you are the teacher, you could say that you "learn" each child through observation.

As you watch a particular child or a group, you discover how the environment is working and get ideas about how to modify it to make it work better for a particular child or for all the children. Observation is the key to implementing curriculum. Every part of any program is built on observation. In addition, observation can have a positive emotional effect on children; they feel appreciated when teachers observe them closely enough to know them well.

There are many benefits to becoming a good observer. Through observing children you learn about their developmental stages, as well as their uniqueness—their likes and dislikes, behavior patterns, how they interact with others and the world around them. You can get insights on how to intervene to enhance the child's learning process. A good observer can even begin to see the world from other perspectives.

When you observe, you *pay attention!* One of the major benefits of observation is that it puts you in the present. It keeps you in touch with the here and now. Observation is more than just watching. It is paying attention with all your senses in order to understand. It is making the invisible visible and also being aware of what's not happening as well as what is. This kind of understanding comes through analyzing and interpreting what you perceive. Skilled observers learn to see with the kind of "ethnographic eyes" that anthropologists use.

How to Observe: Some General Guidelines

There are lots of ways to observe. Some of them involve standing back and staying out of the action and others occur while you are part of what you are observing. Ongoing informal observations can become a good habit. Teachers also need to make more formal observations on occasion, especially when they want to find out something that they can't just casually discover. Some of these observations must occur over time. Some forms these observations take are quick notes, lengthier notes, time samples, event samples, and checklists, to name a few.

Notes can be made on the spot, or remembered later and written down then. Writing is required because, if you don't keep records of what you observe, you forget. Memory alone can't hold all the details sometimes needed. Written records are useful in many ways. One way is by reviewing them over a period of time. When you go back and look again at what you've recorded, sometimes patterns emerge that wouldn't show otherwise.

To truly understand an individual or a group, observations must occur in a variety of settings, situations, and times of day. There's no other way to get a bigger picture. The same is true of observing families. Remember that you can't really know a family if you only see them when they are saying good-bye and hurrying away or when they come back tired and ready to go home and get the next meal ready. For many families, those are two of the worst times of the day. Ideally, to really know a family you should see them in different settings and situations.

For record-keeping purposes it is important to always write down the date and time of an observation (time of day and duration) and the setting, as well as the name and age of the child or children. These kinds of headings should even be on very quick notes written on the run. It can help to also include any additional information such as the specific circumstance. Observing the first day back from a vacation is different from observing the last day before a vacation, for example.

It is important to be respectful at all times. If a child is uncomfortable at being observed, stop. Also, you should be careful to not be intrusive. You don't want any children to feel like they are bugs under a microscope! These are more than just suggestions—they are ethical responsibilities. Children have a right to be protected from embarrassment, stress, or anxiety from observers. They also have the right to have any information collected kept confidential so that their privacy is never violated. That means information is to only be used as part of a learning assignment and children's real names should not be revealed. Parental consent is another consideration. In many observation sites, parents have given blanket written consent. Check with the program where you observe to be sure that you don't need special parental consent and that the teachers and other staff also have given consent to your observing.

The data you gather through observations should be detailed and objective. Seek to describe rather than judge. Record what you actually see in terms of physical behaviors, facial expressions, body movements, and gestures rather than taking short cuts by saying the child is "playing" or is "angry." Show rather than labeling. Someone reading your observation should see what you saw and, if you give accurate details, may be able to interpret the behavior in the same ways that you interpreted it. Yes, interpretation of the objective data is also part of observation, but don't just skip to labeling and interpreting without describing exactly what you are seeing. Context is important. For example, you see the child is rubbing her eyes. You may not know why for sure, but in looking at the child and knowing the context you might be able to guess. Is this a baby who always takes a nap at this time of day? Is this a toddler who is sitting in the sandbox? Have you noticed redness in this child's eyes and you suspect an infection? The eye rubbing is the data. The guess as to its meaning, or why it is happening, is your interpretation. Both are important, but keep them separate. Be aware of which is which.

The goal is to be objective, but that doesn't mean you can ever step out of your own skin. The observer is always part of the picture. Become aware of the effects you are having on what and whom you are observing. Also observe the effects on you of what you see. Notice sore areas and hot spots that the actions of others touch in you. Notice the part of you that is wanting to judge what you are seeing. Notice the part of you that is quick to jump to conclusions. Be aware that those conclusions may be based on false assumptions. Although you try to gather objective data through observations, you can't leave yourself out of it. Separate the objective and subjective. If the subjective in the form of judgments, assumptions, and feelings keeps getting in the way, write it down and acknowledge that it is subjective. Put that piece of paper away and then focus on turning to a more objective mode where you observe what's really happening and interpret it without all the personal issues you've acknowledged and literally put away.

Observation Strategies and Techniques for Understanding Children

1. **Reflections.** One of the simplest kinds of observations is to pay attention to what you see without taking notes and then think about them afterward and write down what you remembered and what you learned.

2. **Running Record Observations.** A running record is a blow-by-blow description of what is happening while it is happening. You write down exactly what you see, first in notes and then in full, complete sentences and paragraphs, separating the objective data from your interpretation of it. Details are important in running record observations. Some running records include interpretations while others don't.

3. **Anecdotal Records.** A contrast to running records, anecdotal records are a short written descriptions of events or a behaviors written down soon after they occur. They can be written as notes immediately after the occurrence and then written up more completely later. Out of seemingly unconnected notes can emerge patterns and answers to questions about a child. Some teachers keep index cards in a pocket always handy to quickly jot down anecdotes when they occur.

4. **Checklists.** A simple assessment tool, checklists come in many forms and are used for a variety of purposes. They involve little writing. Four different kinds are used in the observation activities that follow. An environmental checklist can be used to assess what's in the environment and how it is set up. Another type of environmental checklist can focus on some special quality of the environment—such as the ways in which equity is promoted. Still another type of environmental checklist shows the use and effectiveness of the physical setup by keeping track of who is where every few minutes so you can see some patterns of individual and group use of the various areas and activities. A developmental checklist is a way to get a view of the child's skills at a given time.

5. **Incidents Reports.** Incidents reports record a particular type of repeated occurrence from beginning to finish. The idea is to observe and record everything that happens right before, during, and after each incident. By doing so, you may be able to see patterns that suggest why the incidents occur.

6. **Event Sampling.** This approach focuses on a specific behavior during a specific event, such as separation anxiety during arrival times.

7. **Time Samples.** Time samples are a collection of a few target behaviors of small groups of children to show individual and group patterns.

8. **Mapping.** Mapping is a way of looking at behaviors of a particular child in a play environment and is used most effectively with children who move around a lot, such as mobile infants and toddlers. It can serve a similar purpose to an environmental checklist by helping the observer understand the specifics of how a child functions in the environment.

9. **Journals and Logs.** These can be open-ended written records or forms to fill out recording specifics. Journals may contain all sorts of writing including anecdotal records, running records, and incidents reports. They may also contain drawings or photographs. Sometimes they are used as a communication device between shift staff who care for the same child sequentially, one who is there at the beginning of the day and one who comes in after the first one leaves. Also sometimes they are used as a means of communicating with parents and hearing back from them. More often they are used with infants and toddlers, though sometimes used with older children as well. What's called the daily log is one form of a journal.

Learning Through Observation Activities

This section links observation activities with each chapter of the text.

Chapter 1. Early Childhood Education as a Profession

Directions: Arrange to observe in an early childhood setting. Find a place where you are out of the way and yet can see the room or play yard. Pick five children and observe them for one hour. At the end of the time, fill out the form.

OBSERVATION AND REFLECTION

Date: _____   Time: _____   Duration of Observation: _____

Setting: _____

Directions: Indicate which child is which by giving a first name, initials, or some identifying characteristic such as "red shirt." Then think back to what you observed. Write something that you remember about each child.

Child 1

Child 2

Child 3

Child 4

Child 5

Now write down what you discovered about yourself in regard to these children. Did you find you were attracted to one or two of the children more than the others? If yes, what attracted you? Did you have a harder time thinking of what to write about one or more of them? If yes, why? What did you learn about yourself by doing this observation?

Chapter 2. First Things First: Providing for the Child's Physical Health and Safety

OBSERVING AN ADULT SUPERVISING A GROUP OF YOUNG CHILDREN

Date: _____   Time: _____   Duration of Observation: _____

Setting: _____

Directions: Write a running record of exactly what you see while watching a teacher, caregiver, aide, student, or other adult supervising young children.

Did you see the adult interacting with an individual or small group giving close personal attention while also watching the other children as described in Chapter 2? If yes, describe. If no, explain why you think the person you observed didn't do both.

Did you learn something about the positioning of adults for safe supervision? If yes, describe.

What did you get out of doing this observation?

Chapter 3. Providing for the Child's Emotional Growth and Well-Being Through Communication

ACTIVITY: PRACTICING KEEPING ANECDOTAL RECORDS ON FIVE CHILDREN.

Directions: Write down whatever you see that seems important while observing five children. Remembering what you read in Chapter 2, try to capture what the child communicates both verbally and nonverbally. Make note of what kind of response the child receives when he or she communicates.

ANECDOTAL RECORD

Directions: Write down whatever you see that seems important. Try to capture what the child communicates either through words or other means.

Child 1 (name, initial, or other way of identifying) _____ Approximate age:_____

Date: _____ Time: _____ Setting: _____ Circumstances:_____

Narrative account of what you saw:

ANECDOTAL RECORD

Directions: Write down whatever you see that seems important. Try to capture what the child communicates either through words or other means.

Child 2 (name, initial, or other way of identifying) _____ Approximate age:_____

Date: _____ Time: _____ Setting: _____ Circumstances:_____

Narrative account of what you saw:

ANECDOTAL RECORD

Directions: Write down whatever you see that seems important. Try to capture what the child communicates either through words or other means.

Child 3 (name, initial, or other way of identifying) _____ Approximate age:_____

Date: _____ Time: _____ Setting: _____ Circumstances:_____

Narrative account of what you saw:

ANECDOTAL RECORD

Directions: Write down whatever you see that seems important. Try to capture what the child communicates either through words or other means.

Child 4 (name, initial, or other way of identifying) _____ Approximate age:_____

Date: _____ Time: _____ Setting: _____ Circumstances:_____

Narrative account of what you saw:

ANECDOTAL RECORD

Directions: Write down whatever you see that seems important. Try to capture what the child communicates either through words or other means.

Child 5 (name, initial, or other way of identifying) _____ Approximate age:_____

Date: _____ Time: _____ Setting: _____ Circumstances:_____

Narrative account of what you saw:

Chapter 4. Facilitating Young Children's Work and Play

Activity: Use the form below to observe how five children in an early care and education play-based program use the environment for play.

ENVIRONMENTAL CHECKLIST SHOWING FIVE CHILDREN AT PLAY

Directions: Check where each child is every 5 minutes for half an hour. By keeping track of where these children are periodically you may see some patterns of individual and group behavior. A sample of this activity is in Chapter 12, page 321 of the text.

Date: _____

Time of observation: _____

No. 1   No. 2   No. 3   No. 4   No. 5

Enter the names of the areas down the left side and the first names, initial, or identifying description of the child across the top. Then write the time of observation in the block of the area where the child is when you check each time.

AREAS	Child 1	Child 2	Child 3	Child 4	Child 5

Write here what you discovered by doing this activity:

Chapter 5. Guiding Young Children's Behavior

Activity: Use an Incidents Report to look for aggressive behavior in a particular child.

INCIDENTS REPORT

Directions: Observe a child known to show aggression. Observe for a long enough period of time to see a number of interactions with adults and peers. Watch for incidents of aggression and record what you see using this form.

Age and gender of child: _____

Date: _____ Time: _____ Duration of Observation: _____

Setting: _____

Any special circumstances: _____

Incident 1: What preceded the incident?

What happened during the incident?

What were the results of the aggression?

Were any guidance approaches used by an adult? If yes, describe.

What do you think the child learned from this incident?

Other comments?

Incident 2: What preceded the incident?

What happened during the incident?

What were the results of the aggression?

Were any guidance approaches used by an adult? If yes, describe.

What do you think the child learned from this incident?

Other comments?

Incident 3: What preceded the incident?

What happened during the incident?

What were the results of the aggression?

Were any guidance approaches used by an adult? If yes, describe.

What do you think the child learned from this incident?

Other comments?

Incident 4: What preceded the incident?

What happened during the incident?

What were the results of the aggression?

Were any guidance approaches used by an adult? If yes, describe.

What do you think the child learned from this incident?

Other comments?

Incident 5: What preceded the incident?

What happened during the incident?

What were the results of the aggression?

Were any guidance approaches used by an adult? If yes, describe.

What do you think the child learned from this incident?

Other comments?

Chapter 6. The Teacher as Model

Activity: Equity Checklist to observe how well a program promotes and models equitable approaches to care and education?

EQUITY CHECKLIST FOR EARLY CARE AND EDUCATION PROGRAMS

Score the environment

a lot or almost always = 2	a little or sometimes = 1	none or almost never = 0

Score

____ 1. Do children see themselves and their families represented in the staff, pictures, photos, books, and other materials? Do children hear their language spoken?

____ 2. Is this an inclusive program where diversity is welcomed?

____ 3. Do children see and hear adults interacting with each other in respectful and equitable ways across the lines of color, culture, ethnicity, age, ability, religion, sexual orientation, family make up?

____ 4. Is the staff well-trained in developmentally appropriate practice and how to include culturally appropriate and individually appropriate practices as well?

____ 5. Is there an initial process for finding out what each family wants for their child (or children) in terms of approaches to care and education?

____ 6. Are cultural sensitivity and responsiveness evident, including an ongoing process for communicating with families around differences in ideas about what's best for children?

____ 7. Is there an openness to creating consistency of care and education for each child by adapting the policies and practices of the program to meet each family's deeply held values and the related practices?

____ 8. If the families in the program all appear to be of similar background, is effort made to uncover existing invisible diversity?

____ 9. If the families are of similar background, is effort made to counteract media stereotypes and expose children periodically to people who are different from those they know?

____ Total Points

14–18 The program is well on the road to an equity approach
7–13   Not there yet
0–6   Changes needed to make an equity focused program

What did you learn by doing this activity?

Chapter 7. Modeling Adult Relationships in Early Childhood Settings

Activity: Using an events sampling method of observation at arrival and or departure times to look at adult relationships.

EVENT SAMPLING AT ARRIVAL
AND/OR DEPARTURE TIMES

Directions: Observe in an early childhood setting to see what clues you can pick up as to how welcome parents or other family members feel there. Watch interactions between teachers and parents and note communication, both verbal and nonverbal.

Date: _____ Time: _____ Duration of observation: _____ Setting: _____

Family 1: Arrival or departure? (Circle one.) Describe who brought or picked up the child, behaviors of child, behaviors of family member, and behaviors of teacher. What happened? Give details. What clues do you have that indicated that the family member felt welcome? Any clues that would lead you to believe otherwise?

Family 2: Arrival or departure? (Circle one.) Describe who brought or picked up the child, behaviors of child, behaviors of family member, and behaviors of teacher. What happened? Give details. What clues do you have that indicated that the family member felt welcome? Any clues that would lead you to believe otherwise?

Family 3: Arrival or departure? (Circle one.) Describe who brought or picked up the child, behaviors of child, behaviors of family member, and behaviors of teacher. What happened? Give details. What clues do you have that indicated that the family member felt welcome? Any clues that would lead you to believe otherwise?

Family 4: Arrival or departure? (Circle one.) Describe who brought or picked up the child, behaviors of child, behaviors of family member, and behaviors of teacher. What happened? Give details. What clues do you have that indicated that the family member felt welcome? Any clues that would lead you to believe otherwise?

Chapter 8. Setting Up the Physical Environment

Activity: Using a checklist to assess the patterns of use in an early childhood indoor environment set up for play. See sample and discussion of this activity in Chapter 12 of the text on page 330.

ENVIRONMENTAL CHECKLIST: ASSESSING PATTERNS OF USE IN THE INDOOR ENVIRONMENT

Directions: Observe every 10 minutes who is in what area of the play environment. Write the time of each observation in the spaces across the top. Some play areas have been named down the side, but if they don't fit what you are observing, change the names or add new ones to the spaces below. Also, you can observe outside and name the play spaces and activities there using the blank spaces. Count the boys and girls in each play space and write the numbers under the time of the observation. Observe for 1 hour, if free play lasts that long.

Date of Observation: _____

TIME															
BOYS/GIRLS	B	G	B	G	B	G	B	G	B	G	B	G	B	G
Blocks														
Art Table														
Easels														
Dramatic Play														
Manipulatives														
Music Area														
Book Corner														
Science Table														

Your comments:

What did you learn by doing this activity?

Chapter 9. Creating a Social–Emotional Environment

Activity: Observe the effects of the social–emotional environment on a child using the Running Record Observation form.

Directions: Observe one child for the period of an hour in an early childhood program, taking notes on index cards. Record the time in 10-minute intervals. Write up the notes as soon as possible after the observation in a running record narrative using full sentences and paragraphs.

RUNNING RECORD OBSERVATION

Time	What is actually seen	Meaning of observed behaviors

Page 2

RUNNING RECORD OBSERVATION

Time	What is actually seen	Meaning of observed behaviors

Page 3

RUNNING RECORD OBSERVATION

Time	What is actually seen	Meaning of observed behaviors

Page 4

RUNNING RECORD OBSERVATION

Time	What is actually seen	Meaning of observed behaviors

Page 5

RUNNING RECORD OBSERVATION

Time	What is actually seen	Meaning of observed behaviors

Study your running record observation and see if you can discover the effects on the child of the social–emotional environment as described in Chapter 9. Write about that here.

Chapter 10. Routines

Activity: Observe a *group time* using the time sample sheet below. Choose five children to observe at 3-minute intervals for about half an hour.

TIME SAMPLE

Directions: Write down the time and observe the children in order marking the code representing what each is doing in the time slot going across under the children's names. See Sample in Chapter 12 of the text, page 325.

Codes	
A	Attending to what is going on
P	Participating in what is going on
C	Compliant but not attending or participating
I	Interacting with another child——not attending
S	Self-involved—not attending
T	Trying to get the teacher's attention—not attending
M	Moving away from the group—not attending

Date: _____ Setting: _____

Time	Child 1	Child 2	Child 3	Child 4	Child 5

Chapter 11. Developmental Tasks as the Curriculum: How to Support Children at Each Stage

ANECDOTAL RECORD

Directions: Choose one child and write down whatever you see in the areas of physical, social-emotional, or cognitive skills that the child displayed as explained in Chapter 11, where the specifics of each stage were described.

Child (first name, initial or other way of identifying) _____ Approximate age: _____

Date: _____ Time: _____ Setting: _____ Circumstances: _____

Narrative account of what you saw:

ANECDOTAL RECORD

Directions: Choose one child and write down whatever you see in the areas of physical, social-emotional, or cognitive skills that the child displayed as explained in Chapter 11, where the specifics of each stage were described.

Child (first name, initial or other way of identifying) _____ Approximate age: _____

Date: _____ Time: _____ Setting: _____ Circumstances: _____

Narrative account of what you saw:

ANECDOTAL RECORD

Directions: Choose one child and write down whatever you see in the areas of physical, social-emotional, or cognitive skills that the child displayed as explained in Chapter 11, where the specifics of each stage were described.

Child (first name, initial or other way of identifying) _____ Approximate age: _____

Date: _____ Time: _____ Setting: _____ Circumstances: _____

Narrative account of what you saw:

ANECDOTAL RECORD

Directions: Choose one child and write down whatever you see in the areas of physical, social-emotional, or cognitive skills that the child displayed as explained in Chapter 11, where the specifics of each stage were described.

Child (first name, initial or other way of identifying) _____ Approximate age: _____

Date: _____ Time: _____ Setting: _____ Circumstances: _____

Narrative account of what you saw:

Go back through your anecdotal records and see what behaviors that you recorded that would indicate the stage of development this child is in. Do the stage and age correspond as describe in Chapter 11? This exercise is for practice only—it is not intended as an assessment of the child.

What kinds of supports did you see that facilitated skill building in what you recorded?

Adult support? Write about that.

Environmental support? Write about that.

What did you learn by doing this activity?

Chapter 12. Observing, Recording, and Assessing

Activity: After reading Chapter 12, figure out how you would collect material for a portfolio as an assessment approach for one of the children you have been studying using the various forms of observation and recording. Also think about what you could collect as you continue to observe. Record below some ideas of what this collection might include. At the end write a brief statement about how you might use this collection for making some kind of assessment of the child if you were the teacher of that child.

Chapter 13. Language and Emergent Literacy

Activity: Observing activities for building literacy skills and attitudes. Observe for 2 hours and keep track of the kinds of activities that involve literacy skills that you see. Make a list of what you saw, where you saw it, and how it related to early literacy. Don't just look for actual reading and writing behaviors; go beyond books, pencils, and paper activities. Also include activities that build eye–hand coordination, fine motor control, language exploration including playing with sound, rhyme, rhythm, vocabulary expansion, and uses of symbols of all sorts. List those activities here.

Chapter 14. Providing Developmentally Appropriate Experiences in Math and Science

Activity: Observe in an early care and education program for children under 6. Make notes on how children are learning math and science concepts. Then visit a primary classroom and see in what ways it is the same and in what ways it is different. Write about what you saw and how the approaches to learning and teaching in the two different age groups compared.

Chapter 15. Integrating Art, Music, and Social Studies into a Holistic Curriculum

	RUNNING RECORD OBSERVATION	
Time	What is actually seen	Meaning of observed behaviors

Page 2

RUNNING RECORD OBSERVATION

Time	What is actually seen	Meaning of observed behaviors

Page 3

RUNNING RECORD OBSERVATION

Time	What is actually seen	Meaning of observed behaviors

Reflection Questions

Chapter 1. Early Childhood Education as a Profession

1. Pick one of the four themes of the text—reflective thinking, a multicultural perspective, a holistic approach, and professionalism—and write a short essay giving your views, thoughts, experiences with, or ideas about the theme.

2. Review the ages and stages information, then think of your own ages and stages. Describe how you were or think you were in each of them and say which ones stand out in your mind.

3. Explain both/and thinking in your own terms and give an example.

Chapter 2. First Things First: Providing for the Child's Physical Health and Safety

1. Explain how supervising young children properly keeps them safe and helps them learn at the same time.

2. Make a list of what you can learn about individual children and groups of children by observing them.

3. When young children argue, adults often settle the argument for them. An alternative approach is to stay with them, encouraging them to settle the argument themselves. What can they learn from the first approach? What can they learn from the second approach?

4. Discuss the difference between teaching obedience and teaching cooperation.

Chapter 3. Providing for the Child's Emotional Growth and Well-Being Through Communication

1. Often children's strong feelings trigger memories and feelings in adults, who then try to make the child's feelings go away. Discuss why it is important from some cultural perspectives to validate those feelings. Explain why someone from a different culture might not see validation as important.

2. What do you know about helping young children separate from family members when dropped off at school or child care? Discuss some strategies for helping young children cope with whatever feelings they may have, whether of anxiety, fear, anger, or confusion.

3. Discuss how feelings are linked to cognitive development.

Chapter 4. Facilitating Young Children's Work and Play

1. The teacher shouldn't be the star of the show, according to the text. What does that mean? What are your ideas and feelings about that statement?

2. What are some strategies to make play accessible to all children including those with disabilities?

3. Explain how children learn through play.

Chapter 5. Guiding Young Children's Behavior

1. How would you teach a child to hang up her coat if she didn't seem to want to?

2. What are limits? Why do children need them? What does testing the limits mean? Write a short essay explaining limits for young children and incorporate the answer to the question above.

3. If behavior is communication, can you give an example of when a child's misbehavior is trying to tell you something? Explain.

Chapter 6. The Teacher as Model

1. What are some approaches early childhood educators can take in their programs to reduce violence in the society?

2. What are ways that adults model positive behaviors in the face of equity issues?

3. Explain what an emergent curriculum is and give an example.

Chapter 7. Modeling Adult Relationships in Early Childhood Settings

1. Consider the term authenticity. Think about why the text says adults should be authentic around young children. What does that mean? Can you give some examples of authenticity in adults in an early childhood setting?

2. What are some ways that the early childhood educator's role differs from that of a parent?

3. Discuss parent–teacher relationships in terms of modeling for children.

Chapter 8. Setting Up the Physical Environment

1. What does the statement, "The environment is a teacher" mean?

2. What does it mean when an environment is "developmentally appropriate"? Give an example of developmental appropriateness. Give an example of something in the environment is developmentally inappropriate.

3. What are some ways to adapt the environment in a full inclusion program for children with special needs or disabilities?

Chapter 9. Creating a Social–Emotional Environment

1. What does it mean for an adult to treat children with respect? Give an example of an adult behavior that shows respect.

2. Write a short essay on how warmth, nurturance, acceptance, protection, and responsiveness relate to an appropriate social–emotional environment and why continuity is also needed.

3. What do you understand about the differing priorities of independence or interdependence? Can you explain those priorities? Can you give examples of behaviors that relate to each?

Chapter 10. Routines

1. Caregiving is curriculum. What does that statement mean? Explain and give examples.

2. Discuss why a person studying to be a primary teacher might need to learn about those essential activities of daily living called caregiving routines (i.e., diapering, feeding, grooming, dressing).

3. What is a transition? Give an example of a transition. Create a list of ways to make the transition in your example go smoothly.

Chapter 11. Developmental Tasks as the Curriculum: How to Support Children at Each Stage

1. Pick two of the eight stages of development explained in this chapter and compare how typically developing children in each of those stages might differ in physical, social–emotional, and cognitive development.

2. Why is it important to know about developmental stages?

3. Write a short essay about some of the issues that can arise over using developmental charts.

Chapter 12. Observing, Recording, and Assessing

1. How might you use a series of observations of specific incidents, such as aggressive incidents, to understand behavioral patterns?

2. Discuss some of the issues around assessing children.

3. Explain what a portfolio is and how you might use one.

Chapter 13. Language and Emergent Literacy

1. Discuss how some children risk losing their home language when they come to an English-only early childhood program.

2. What are some ways to facilitate language development in 3-, 4-, and 5-year-olds?

3. What is emergent literacy and how does it differ from a reading-readiness approach?

Chapter 14. Providing Developmentally Appropriate Experiences in Math and Science

1. What are some science materials and activities that provide hands-on learning experiences for young children?

2. What are some manipulative math materials and activities to help young children learn basic mathematical concepts?

3. Write a short essay on what relationship math and science have to each other and why they are together in a single chapter.

Chapter 15. Integrating Art, Music, and Social Studies into a Holistic Curriculum

1. What do children gain from art experiences? Give some examples.

2. What are some ways that children can learn about and experience music?

3. Social studies starts with learning about the self and moves from self to others. Explain that statement and why it is a progression that makes sense to use with young children. Could there be a different progression that also makes sense? If yes, explain.

4. What is a topic web and what is it used for?

Resources

Magazines and Newsletters

Child Care Information Exchange
Child Care Plus
Child Health ALERT
Exceptional Children
Exceptional Parent
Scholastic Early Childhood Today
Teaching Exceptional Children

Journals

Periodicals Relevant to Child Development Teachers and Students

American Educational Research Journal
American Psychologist
Applied Psycholinguistics
British Journal of Developmental Psychology
Child Abuse and Neglect
Child and Youth Care Quarterly
Child Development
Child Development Abstracts and Bibliography
Childhood Education
Child Psychiatry and Human Development
Clinical Pediatrics
Contemporary Educational Psychology
Developmental Psychology
Developmental Review
Early Childhood Research Quarterly
Genetic, Social, and General Psychology Monographs
Harvard Educational Review
Human Development
Infant Behavior and Development
International Journal of Behavior Development
Journal of Abnormal Child Psychology
Journal of the American Academy of Child and Adolescent Psychiatry
Journal of Behavior Genetics
Journal of Clinical Child Psychology
Journal of Divorce
Journal of Educational Psychology

Journal of Experimental Child Psychology
Journal of Genetic Psychology
Journal of Marriage and the Family
Journal of Youth and Adolescence
Merrill-Palmer Quarterly
Monographs of the Society for Research in Child Development
Pre- and Perinatal Psychology Journal
Psychological Bulletin
Psychological Review
Review of Educational Research
Young Children
Zero to Three

Cross-Cultural Psychological Research

International Journal of Behavioral Development
International Journal of Intercultural Relations
International Journal of Psychology
Journal of Cross-Cultural Psychology
Psychology and Developing Societies

Other Journals with an International or Cross-Cultural Perspective

European Journal of Social Psychology
Hispanic Journal of Behavioral Sciences
Inter-American Journal of Psychology
Journal of Social Psychology
OMEP International Journal of Early Childhood

Canadian Journals

Canadian Children
Canadian Journal of Education
Canadian Journal of Research in Early Childhood Education Interaction

Additional Readings for Diversity Information

Nonfiction

Akbar, Na'im. *Breaking the Chains of Psychological Slavery.* Tallahasee, Florida: Mind Productions, 1996.

Akbar, Na'im. *The Community of Self.* Tallahasee, Florida: Mind Productions, 1985.

Akbar, Na'im. *Light from Ancient Africa.* Tallahasee, Florida: Mind Productions, 1994.

Alderete-Baker, Elena. "Internalized Achievement-Related Motives of Native American Women." Unpublished Ph.D. Dissertation, 1998.

Allen, Paula Gunn. *Off the Reservation.* Boston: Beacon Press, 1998.

Anderson, P. "Explaining Intercultural Differences in Nonverbal Communication." In *Intercultural Communication: A Reader,* edited by L. Samavar and R. Porter. Belmont, Calif.: Wadsworth, 1994.

Anderson, P., and Emily S. Fenichel. *Serving Culturally Diverse Families of Infants and Toddlers with Disabilities.* Washington, D.C.: National Center for Clinical Infant Programs, 1989, ED 318174.

Banks, James A. *Cultural Diversity and Education.* Boston: Allyn and Bacon, 2001.

Bell, Derrick. *Faces at the Bottom of the Well: The Permanence of Racism.* New York: Basic Books, 1992.

Bernhard, Judith K., Marlinda Freire, Fidelia Torres, and Suparna Nirdosh. "Latin Americans in a Canadian Primary School: Perspectives of Parents, Teachers and Children on Cultural Identity and Academic Achievement." *Canadian Journal of Regional Science* (Spring/Summer 1997): 217–137.

Bernheimer, Susan. "New Possibilities for Early Chidlhood Education." Stories from *Our Nontraditional Students.* New York: Peter Lang, 2003.

Bernard, Judith, Marie Louise Lefebvre, Gyda Chud, and Rika Lange. *Paths to Equity: Cultural, Linguistic, and Racial Diversity in Canadian Early Childhood Education.* Toronto: York Lanes Press, 1995.

Bhavnagri, Navaz, and Janet Gonzalez-Mena. "The Cultural Context of Caregiving." *Childhood Education 74,* no. 1 (Fall, 1997): 2–8.

Bowman, Barbara T., and Frances M. Stott. "Understanding Development in a Cultural Context: The Challenge for Teachers." In *Diversity and Developmentally Appropriate Practices: Challenges for Early Childhood Education,* edited by Bruce L. Mallory and Rebecca S. New. New York: Teachers College Press, 1994, 119–133.

Brazelton, T. Berry. "A Child Oriented Approach to Toilet Training." *Pediatrics 29,* no. 1 (January 1962): 121–128.

Bredekamp, Sue, ed. *Developmentally Appropriate Practice in Early Childhood Programs Serving Children from Birth Through Age 8.* Washington, D.C.: National Association for the Education of Young Children, 1997.

Brody, Hugh. *The Other Side of Eden: Hunters, Farmers, and the Shaping of the World.* New York: North Point Press, 2001.

Brown, Joseph E. *The Spiritual Legacy of the American Indian.* New York: Crossroad Publishing, 1982.

Bruno, Holly Elissa. "Hearing Parents in Every Language: An Invitation to ECE Professionals." *Child Care Information Exchange,* #153 (September/October 2003): 58–60.

Cajete, Gregory. *Look to the Mountain: An Ecology of Indigenous Education.* Durango, Colo.: Kivaki Press, 1994.

Cannella, Gaile Sloan. *Deconstructing Early Childhood Education: Social Justice and Revolution.* New York: Peter Lang, 1997.

Carroll, Raymonde. *Cultural Misunderstandings: The French-American Experience.* Chicago: University of Chicago Press, 1988.

Carter, Margie. "Face to Face Communication: Understanding and Strengthening the Partnership." *Child Care Information Exchange 60* (1988): 21–25.

Chan, J. "Chinese Intelligence." In *The Handbook of Chinese Psychology,* edited by M. H. Bond. Hong Kong: Oxford University Press, 1996.

Chang, Hedy. *Affirming Children's Roots: Cultural and Linguistic Diversity in Early Care and Education.* San Francisco: California Tomorrow, 1993.

Chao, R. "Beyond parental control and authoritarian parenting style: Understanding Chinese parenting through the cultural notion of training." *Child Development 65* (1994): 1111–1119.

Chen, X., K. Rubin, G. Gen, P. Hastings, H. Chen, and S. Stewart. "Child-rearing attitudes and behavioral inhibition in Chinese and Canadian toddlers: A cross-cultural study." *Developmental Psychology 34,* no. 4 (1998): 677–686.

Child Care Health Program. *Serving Biracial and Multiethnic Children and Their Families.* Berkeley, Calif.: The Child Care Health Program, 2003.

Chud, Gyda, and R. Fahlman. *Early Childhood Education for a Multicultural Society: A Handbook for Educators.* Vancouver, B.C.: Pacific Educational Press, 1990.

Coll, Cynthia Garcia, Gontran Lamberty, Renee Jenkins, Harriet Pipes McAdoo, Keith Crnic, Barbara Hanna Wasik, and Heidie Vazquez Garcia. "An Integrative Model for the Study of Developmental Competencies in Minority Children." *Child Development 67* (1996): 1891–1914.

Cronin, Sharon, Louise Derman-Sparks, Sharon Henry, Cirecie Olatunji, and Stacey York. *Future Vision, Present Work: Learning from the Culturally Relevant Anti-Bias Leadership Project.* St. Paul, Minn.: Redleaf, 1998.

Cummins, Jim. Negotiating Identities: *Education for Empowerment in a Diverse Society.* Ontario, Calif.: California Association for Bilingual Education, 1996.

DeLoache, Judy and Alma Gottlieb. *A World of Babies: Imagined Childcare Guides for Seven Societies.* New York: Cambridge University Press, 2000.

Delpit, Lisa. *Other People's Children: Cultural Conflict in the Classroom.* New York: The New Press, 1995.

Delpit, Lisa. "The Silenced Dialogue: Power and Pedagogy in Educating Other People's Children." *Harvard Educational Review 58,* no. 3 (1988).

Delpit, Lisa, and Joanne Kilgour Dowdy, eds. *The Skin That We Speak.* New York: The New Press, 2002.

Derman-Sparks, Louise. "The Process of Culturally Sensitive Care." In *Infant/Toddler Caregiving: A Guide to Culturally Sensitive Care,* edited by Peter Mangione. Sacramento: Far West Laboratory and California Department of Education, 1995, 39–73.

Derman-Sparks, Louise, and Carol Brunson Phillips. *Teaching/Learning Anti-racism.* New York: Teachers College Press, 1997.

Derman-Sparks, Louise, and the ABC Task Force. *Anti-Bias Curriculum: Tools for Empowering Young Children.* Washington, D.C.: National Association for the Education of Young Children, 1989.

Dung, Trinh Ngoc. "Understanding Asian Families: A Vietnamese Perspective." *Children Today* (March/April 1984): 10–13.

Edwards, Carolyn Pope, Lella Gandini, and Donatella Giovaninni. "The Contrasting Developmental Timetables of Parents and Preschool Teachers in Two Cultural Communities." In *Parents' Cultural Belief Systems,* edited by Sara Harkness and Charles M. Super. New York: Guiliford, 1996, 270–288.

Edwards, Patricia, Kathleen L. Fear, and Margaret A. Gallego. "Role of Parents in Responding to Issues of Linguistic and Cultural Diversity." In *Meeting the Challenge of Linguistic and Cultural Diversity in Early Childhood Education,* edited by Eugene E. Garcia and Barry McLaughlin, with Bernard Spokek and Olivia N. Saracho. New York: Teachers College Press, 1995, 141–153.

Eggers-Pierola, Costanze. *Connections and Commitments: A Latino-based Framework for Early Childhood Educators.* Newton, Mass.: Educational Development Center, 2002.

Ehling, Marta Borbon. "The Mexican American (El Chicano)." In *Culture and Childrearing,* edited by Ann L. Clark. Philadelphia: F. A. Davis Company, 1981, 192–209.

Ellison, Sharon. *Don't Be So Defensive!* Kansas City, Mo.: Andrews McMeel, 1998.

Fadiman, Anne. *The Spirit Catches You and You Fall Down: A Hmong Child, Her American Doctors, and the Collision of Two Cultures.* New York: Noonday Press, 1997.

Fantini, Mario D., and Rene Cardenas, eds. *Parenting in a Multicultural Society.* New York: Longman, 1980.

Fasoli, Lyn, and Janet Gonzalez-Mena. "Let's Be Real: Authenticity in Child Care." *Exchange,* March, 1997.

Fenichel, Emily S., and Linda Eggbeer. *Preparing Practitioners to Work with Infants, Toddlers, and Their Families: Issues and Recommendations for the Professions.* Arlington, Va.: National Center for Clinical Infant Programs, 1990.

Fernea, Elizabeth Warnock. *Children in the Muslim Middle East.* Austin: University of Texas Press, 1995.

Fillmore, Lily Wong. "Luck, Fish Seeds, and Second-Language Learning." In *On Becoming a Language Educator,* edited by Christine Pearson Casanave and Sandra R. Schecter. Mahwah, N.J.: Lawrence Erlbaum, 1997.

Fisher, Roger, and William Ury. *Getting to Yes: Negotiating Agreement Without Giving In.* New York: Penguin Books, 1991.

Freeman, David E., and Yvonnne S. Freeman. *Between Worlds: Access to Second Language Acquisition.* Portsmouth, N.H.: Heinemann, 1994.

Galinsky, Ellen. "From Our President: Why Are Some Parent/Teacher Partnerships Clouded with Difficulties?" *Young Children 45,* no. 5 (July 1990): 2–3, 38–39.

Gandini, Lella and Carolyn Pope, eds. *Bambini: The Italian Approach to Infant/Toddler Care.* New York: Teachers College Press, 2001.

Gao, G., S. Ting-Toomey, and W. Gudykunst. "Chinese communication processes." In *The Handbook of Chinese Psychology,* edited by M. H. Bond. Hong Kong: Oxford University Press, 1996, 280–293.

Garcia, Eugene E. *Student Cultural Diversity: Understanding and Meeting the Challenge,* 2nd Edition. New York: Houghton Mifflin, 1999.

Garcia, Eugene E., and Barry McLaughlin, eds., with Bernard Spokek and Olivia N. Saracho. *Meeting the Challenge of Linguistic and Cultural Diversity in Early Childhood Education.* New York: Teachers College Press, 1995.

Gardner, Howard. *Frames of Mind.* New York: Basic Books, 1983.

_____. To Open Minds: *Chinese Clues to the Dilemma of Contemporary Education.* New York: Basic Books, 1989.

Genishi, Celia, and Margaret Borrego Brainard. "Assessment of Bilingual Children: A Dilemma Seeking Solutions." In *Meeting the Challenge of Linguistic and Cultural Diversity in Early Childhood Education,* edited by Eugene E. Garcia and Barry McLaughlin, with Bernard Spokek and Olivia N. Saracho. New York: Teachers College Press, 1995, 49–62.

Gonzalez, Doris. *Hablemos de Niños.* Caguas, Puerto Rico: Impresos Taino, 2001.

Gonzalez-Mena, Janet. "Cross Cultural Conferences." *Exchange,* July, 1997.

_____. "Cultural Sensitivity in Routine Caregiving Tasks." In *Infant/Toddler Caregiving: A Guide to Culturally Sensitive Care,* edited by Peter Mangione. Sacramento: Far West Laboratory and California Department of Education, 1995, 12–19.

_____. "Dialogue to Understanding Across Cultures." *Exchange* (July 1999): 6–8.

_____. "Do You Have Cultural Tunnel Vision?" *Child Care Information Exchange* (July/August 1991): 29–31.

_____. "Taking a Culturally Sensitive Approach in Infant-Toddler Programs." *Young Children 47,* no. 2 (January 1992): 4–9.

_____. *The Child in the Family and the Community.* New York: Merrill, 2001.

_____. "The Man Who Ordered a Tortilla and Got an Omelette." Minneapolis: Family Information Services, 1995, M, O, 5–6.

_____. "Understanding the Parent's Perspective: Independence or Interdependence?" *Exchange.* September, 1997.

Gonzalez-Mena, Janet, and Judith K. Bernhard. "Out-of-Home Care of Infants and Toddlers: A Call for Cultural and Linguistic Continuity." *Interaction 12,* no. 2, Summer, 1998.

Gonzalez-Mena, Janet, and Navaz Bhavnagri. "Diversity and Infant/Toddler Caregiving." *Young Children,* 1999.

Gonzalez-Mena, Janet, and Anne Stonehouse. *Making Links: A Collaborative Approach to Planning and Practice in Early Childhood Services,* Castle Hills, NSW, Australia: Pademelon Press, 2004.

Gonzalez-Mena, Janet, and Anne Stonehouse. "In the Child's Best Interests." *Child Care Information Exchange* (November 1995): 17–20.

Greenberg, Polly. "Teaching About Native Americans or Teaching About People, Including Native Americans?" *Young Children 47,* no. 6 (September 1992): 27–30, 79–80.

Greenfield, Patricia, Blanca Quiroz, and Catherine Raeff. "Cross-cultural Conflict and Harmony in the Social Construction of the Child." In *New Directions for Child and Adolescent Development,* S. Harkness, C. Raeff, and C. M. Super, eds. San Francisco: Jossey-Bass, 2000, pp. 93-108.

Greenfield, Patricia, and Rodney R. Cocking. *Cross Cultural Roots of Minority Child Development,* Hillside, N.J.: Lawrence Erlbaum, 1994.

Greenman, Jim. "Living in the Real World: Diversity and Conflict." *Exchange* (October 1989): 11.

Grishaber, Susan, and Gaile S. Cannella. *Embracing Identities in Early Childhood Education: Diversity and Possibilities.* New York: Teachers College Press, 2001.

Gudykunst, William B., ed. *Intercultural Communication Theory: Current Perspectives.* Beverly Hills, Calif.: Sage, 1983.

Hakuta, Kenji. *Mirror of Language.* New York: Basic Books, 1986.

Hale, Janice E. "An African-American Early Childhood Education Program: Visions for Children." In *Reconceptualizing the Early Childhood Curriculum: Beginning the Dialogue,* edited by Shirley A. Kessler and Beth Blue Swadener. New York: Teachers College Press, 1992, 205–224.

_____. *Black Children: Their Roots, Culture and Learning Styles.* Baltimore: Johns Hopkins University Press, 1986.

_____. "The Transmission of Cultural Values to Young African American Children." *Young Children 46,* no. 6 (September 1991): 7–15.

Hall, Edward T. *Beyond Culture.* Garden City, N.Y.: Anchor Books, 1977.

Harkness, Sara, and Charles M. Super, eds. *Parents' Cultural Belief Systems.* New York: Guiliford, 1996.

Harwood, Robin L., Joan G. Miller, and Nydia Lucca Irizarry. *Culture and Attachment: Perceptions of the Child in Context.* New York: Guilford Press, 1995.

Heath, Shirley Brice. *Ways with Words: Language, Life and Work in Communities and Classrooms.* Cambridge, Mass.: Cambridge University Press, 1983.

Hildebrand, Verna, Lillian A. Phenice, Mary M. Gray, and Rebecca P. Hines. *Knowing and Serving Diverse Families.* Englewood Cliffs, N.J.: Prentice-Hall, 1996.

hooks, bell. *Rock my Soul, Black People and Self-Esteem.* New York: Atria, 2003.

_____. *Killing Rage: Ending Racism.* New York: Holt, 1995.

Hopson, Darlene Powell, and Derek S. Hopson. *Different and Wonderful: Raising Black Children in a Race-Conscious Society.* New York: Prentice-Hall, 1990.

Hyun, Eunsook. *Making Sense of Developmentally and Culturally Appropritate Practice (DCAP) in Early Childhood Education.* New York: Peter Lang, 1998.

Jipson, Janice. "Extending the Discourse on Developmental Appropriateness: A Developmental Perspective." *Early Education and Development 2,* no. 2 (1991): 95–108.

Johnson-Powell, Gloria, and Joe Yamamoto, eds. *Transcultural Child Development.* New York: Wiley, 1997.

Johnson, David and Roger Johnson. "Cutlral Diversity and Cooperative Learing." In *Cooperative Learning and Strategies for Inclusion,* 2nd Edition, edited by J. W. Putname. Baltimore: Brookes, 1998.

Jones, Elizabeth. *Teaching Adults: An Active Learning Approach.* Washington, D.C.: National Association for the Education of Young Children, 1987.

Jones, Elizabeth, and Louise Derman-Sparks. "Meeting the Challenge of Diversity." *Young Children 47,* no. 2 (January 1992): 12–18.

Jones, Elizabeth, and John Nimo. *Emergent Curriculum.* Washington D.C.: National Association for the Education of Young Children, 1994.

Kagiticibasi, Cigdem. *Family and Human Development Across Cultures.* Mahwah, N.J.: Erlbaum, 1996.

Katz, Lilian. "Child Development Knowledge and Teacher Preparation: Confronting Assumptions." *Early Childhood Research Quarterly 11,* no. 2 (1996): 135–146.

Katz, Lilian G. *Talks with Teachers.* Washington, D.C.: National Association for the Education of Young Children, 1977.

Kawagley, A. Oscar. *A Yupiaz Worldview: A Pathway to Ecology and Spirit.* Prospect Heights, Ill.: Waveland Press, 1995.

Kessler, Shirley A., and Beth B. Swaderner. *Reconceptualizing the Early Childhood Curriculum: Beginning the Dialogue.* New York: Teacher's College Press, 1992.

Kincheloe, Joe L., Shirley R. Steinberg, Nelson M. Rodriguez, and Ronald E. Chennault, eds. *White Reign: Deploying Whiteness in America.* New York: St. Martin's Press, 1998.

Kitano, Margie K. "Early Childhood Education for Asian American Children." *Young Children 35,* no. 2 (January 1980): 13–26.

Kitayama, S., H. Markus, and Matsumoto. "Culture, Self, and Emotion: A Cultural Perspective on 'Self-conscious' Emotions." In *Self-conscious emotions: The psychology of shame, guilt, embarrassment, and pride,* edited by J. P. Tangeny and K. W. Fischer. New York: Guilford Press, 1995.

Knight, George P., Martha E. Bernal, and Gustavo Carlo. "Socialization and the Development of Cooperative, Competitive, and Individualistic Behaviors Among Mexican American Children." In *Meeting the Challenge of Linguistic and Cultural Diversity in Early Childhood Education,* edited by Eugene E. Garcia and Barry McLaughlin, with Bernard Spokek and Olivia N. Saracho. New York: Teachers College Press, 1995, 85–102.

Ladson-Billings, Gloria. *The Dreamkeepers: Successful Teachers of African American Children.* San Francisco: Jossey-Bass, 1994.

Lee, Dorothy. *Freedom and Culture.* New York: Prentice-Hall, 1959.

Lee, Fong Yun. "Asian Parents as Partners." *Young Children 50,* no. 3 (March 1995): 4–8.

Lee, Joann. *Asian Americans.* New York: New Press, 1992.

Lee, K., C. Cameron, F. Xu, G. Fu, and J. Board. "Chinese and Canadian Children's Evaluations of Lying and Truth Telling: Similarities and Differences in the Context of Pro- and Antisocial Behaviors." *Child Development 68,* no. 5 (1997): 924–934.

Lefley, H., and P. Pedersen, eds. *Cross-Cultural Training for Mental Health Professionals.* Springfield, Ill.: Charles C. Thomas, 1986.

LeVine, Robert A. "A Cross-Cultural Perspective on Parenting." In *Parenting in a Multicultural Society,* edited by Mario D. Fantini and R. Cardenas. New York: Longman, 1980, 17–26.

_____. "Child Rearing as Cultural Adaptation." In *Culture and Infancy: Variations in the Human Experience,* edited by P. Herbert Leiderman, Steven R. Tulkin, and Anne Rosenfeld. New York: Academic Press, 1977.

LeVine, Robert A., Sarah LeVine, P. Herbert Leiderman, T. Berry Brazelton, Suzanne Dixon, Amy Richan, and Constant H. Keefer. *Child Care and Culture: Lessons from Africa.* Cambridge University Press, 1994.

Lewis, C. C. *Educating Hearts and Minds: Reflections on Japanese Preschool and Elementary Education.* New York: Cambridge University Press, 1995.

Lieberman, Alicia F. "Concerns of Immigrant Families." In *Infant/Toddler Caregiving: A Guide to Culturally Sensitive Care,* edited by Peter Mangione. Sacramento: Far West Laboratory and California Department of Education, 1995, 28–37.

Liederman, P. Herbert, Steven R. Tulkin, and Anne Rosenfeld. *Culture and Infancy: Variations in the Human Experience.* New York: Academic Press, 1977.

Lin, C. Y., and V. Fu. "A Comparison of Child-rearing Practices among Chinese, Immigrant Chinese, and Caucasian-American Parents." *Child Development 61* (1990): 429–433.

Little Soldier, Lee. "Working with Native American Children." *Young Children 47,* no. 6 (September 1992): 15–21.

Lubeck, Sally. "Deconstructing 'Child Development Knowledge' and 'Teacher Preparation.'" *Early Childhood Research Quarterly 11,* no. 2 (1996): 147–168.

_____. *The Sandbox Society: Early Education in Black and White America.* Philadelphia: Falmer Press, 1985.

Lynch, Eleanor W., and Marci J. Hanson. *Developing Cross-Cultural Competence: A Guide for Working with Young Children and Their Families.* Baltimore: Paul H. Brookes, 1992.

Makin, Laurie, Julie Campbell, and Criss Jones Diaz. *One Childhood Many Languages.* Pymble, NSW, Australia: HarperEducational, 1995.

Mallory, Bruce L., and Rebecca S. New, eds. *Diversity and Developmentally Appropriate Practices: Challenges for Early Childhood Education.* New York: Teachers College Press, 1994.

Mangione, Peter, ed. *Infant/Toddler Caregiving: A Guide to Culturally Sensitive Care.* Sacramento: Far West Laboratory and California Department of Education, 1995.

Matthiessen, Neba. The Hmong: *A Multicultural Study.* Fairfield, Calif.: Fairfield-Suisun Unified School District, 1987.

McCall, Nathan. *Makes Me Wanna Holler.* New York: Vintage Books, 1994.

McGoldrick, Monica, Joe Giordano, and John K. Pearce, eds. *Ethnicity and Family Therapy,* 2nd Edition. New York: Guilford Press, 1996.

McIntosh, Peggy. "White Privilege and Male Privilege: A Personal Account of Coming to See Correspondences Through Work in Women's Studies." Working Paper no. 189, Wellesley College Center for Research on Women, Wellesley, Mass., 1988.

McLoyd, Vonnie. "The Impact of Economic Hardship on Black Families and Children: Psychological Distress, Parenting, and Socioemotional Development." *Child Development 61* (1990): 311–346.

Medicine, Beatrice. "Child Socialization Among Native Americans: The Lakota (Sioux) in Cultural Context." *Wicazo Sa Review 1,* no. 2 (Fall 1985): 23–28.

Miller, P., A. Wiley, H. Gung, and C. H. Liang. "Personal Storytelling as a Medium of Socialization in Chinese and American Families." *Child Development 68,* no. 3 (1997): 557–567.

Miner, Barbara. "Teachers, Culture, and Power: An Interview with African-American Educator Lisa Delpit." *Rethinking Schools* (March/April 1992): 14–16.

Mistry, Jayanthi. "Culture and Learning in Infancy." In *Infant/Toddler Caregiving: A Guide to Culturally Sensitive Care,* edited by Peter Mangione. Sacramento: Far West Laboratory and California Department of Education, 1995, 20–26.

Morelli, Guilda, Barbara Rogoff, and David Oppenheim. "Cultural Variation in Infants' Sleeping Arrangements: Questions of Independence." *Developmental Psychology 28,* no. 4 (July 1992): 604–619.

Morrow, Robert D. "Cultural Differences—Be Aware!" *Academic Therapy 23,* no. 2 (November 1987).

_____. "What's in a Name? In Particular, a Southeast Asian Name?" *Young Children 44,* no. 6 (September 1989): 20–23.

Native American Parent Preschool Curriculum Guide. Oakland, Calif.: Office of Native American Programs, Division of Educational Development and Services, 1986.

Neihardt, John G. *Black Elk Speaks.* New York: Pocket Books, 1972.

Neugebauer, Bonnie, ed. *Alike and Different: Exploring Our Humanity with Young Children.* Washington, D.C.: National Association for the Education of Young Children, 1992.

New, Rebecca S., and Amy L. Richman. "Maternal Beliefs and Infant Care Practices in Italy and the United States." In *Parents' Cultural Belief Systems,* edited by Sara Harkness and Charles M. Super. New York: Guilford, 1996, 385–404.

Nugent, J. Kevin. "Cross-Cultural Studies of Child Development: Implications for Clinicians." *Zero to Three 15,* no. 2 (October/November 1994).

Patterson, Monica Beatriz Demello. "America's Racial Unconscious: The Invisibility of Whiteness." In *White Reign: Deploying Whiteness in America,* edited by Joe L. Kincheloe, Shirley R. Steinberg, Nelson M. Rodriguez, and Ronald E. Chennault. New York: St. Martin's Press, 1998, 103–122.

Pence, Alan R. "Reconceptualizing ECCD in the Majority World: One Minority World Perspective." *International Journal of Early Childhood 30,* no. 2 (1998): 19–30.

Phillips, Carol Brunson. "*Culture:* A Process That Empowers." In *Infant/Toddler Caregiving: A Guide to Culturally Sensitive Care,* edited by Peter Mangione. Sacramento: Far West Laboratory and California Department of Education, 1995, 2–9.

_____. "Nurturing Diversity for Today's Children and Tomorrow's Leaders." *Young Children 43,* no. 2 (1988): 42–47.

_____. "The Movement of African-American Children Through Sociocultural Contexts: A Case of Conflict Resolution." In *Diversity and Developmentally Appropriate Practices: Challenges for Early Childhood Education,* edited by Bruce L. Mallory and Rebecca S. New. New York: Teachers College Press, 1994, 137–154.

Phillips, Carol Brunson, and Renetta M. Cooper. "Cultural Dimensions of Feeding Relationships." *Zero to Three* (June 1992): 10–13.

Powell, Douglas R. "Day Care As a Family Support System." In *America's Family Support Programs,* edited by Sharon Lynn Kagan, Douglas R. Powell, Edward F. Zigler, and B. Weissbourd. New Haven: Yale University Press, 1987, 115–132.

Price, William F., and Richley H. Crapo. *Cross-Cultural Perspectives in Introductory Psychology.* Belmont, California: Wadsworth, 1999.

Procidano, Mary E., and Celia B. Fisher, eds. *Contemporary Families: A Handbook for School Professionals.* New York: Teachers College Press, 1992.

Rael, Joseph. *Being and Vibration.* Tulsa: Council Oak Books, 1993.

Ramirez, M., and A. Castenada. *Cultural Democracy, Bicognitive Development and Education.* New York: Academic Press, 1974.

Ramsey, Patricia, and Louise Derman-Sparks. "Viewpoint: Multicultural Education Reaffirmed." *Young Children 39,* no. 2 (January 1992): 10–11.

Rashid, H. B. "Promoting Biculturalism in Young African-American Children." *Young Children 39,* no. 2 (January 1984): 12–23.

Rogoff, Barbara. *Apprenticeship in Thinking.* New York: Oxford University Press, 1990.

_____. *The Cultural Nature of Human Development.* New York: Oxford University Press, 2003.

Root, Maria, Christine Ho, and Stanley Sue. "Issues in the Training of Counselors for Asian Americans." In *Cross-Cultural Training for Mental Health Professionals,* edited by H. Lefley and P. Pedersen. Springfield, Ill.: Charles C. Thomas, 1986.

Ross, Allen C. (Ehanamani). *Mitakuye Oyasin: We Are All Related.* Denver: Wichoni Waste, 1989.

Russell, J. A., and M. S. M. Yik. "Emotion Among the Chinese." In *The Handbook of Chinese Psychology*, edited by M. H. Bond. Hong Kong: Oxford University Press, 1996, 166–188.

Sandoval, M., and M. De La Roza. "A Cultural Perspective for Serving the Hispanic Client." In *Cross-Cultural Training for Mental Health Professionals,* edited by H. Lefley and P. Pedersen. Springfield, Ill.: Charles C. Thomas, 1986.

Saracho, Olivia N., and Bernard Spokek. "Preparing Teachers for Early Childhood Programs." In *Meeting the Challenge of Linguistic and Cultural Diversity in Early Childhood Education,* edited by Eugene E. Garcia and Barry McLaughlin. New York: Teachers College Press, 1995.

Shick, Lyndall. *Understanding Temperament.* Seattle: Parenting Press, 1998.

Sholtys, Katherine Cullen. "A New Language, A New Life: Recommendations for Teachers of Non-English-Speaking Children Newly Entering the Program." *Young Children 44,* no. 3 (March 1989): 76–77.

Siraj-Blatchford, Iram and Priscilla Clarke. *Supporting Identity, Diversity and Language in the Early Years.* Philadelphia: Open University Press, 2000.

Slapin, Beverly, and Doris Seale. *Books Without Bias: Through Indian Eyes.* Berkeley: Oyate, 1988.

Small, Meredith. *Our Babies, Ourselves: How Biology and Culture Shape the Way We Parent.* New York: Anchor Books, 1998.

Snowden, Lonnie R. "Toward Evaluation of Black Psycho-Social Competence." In *The Pluralistic Society,* edited by Stanley Sue and Thom Moore. New York: Human Sciences Press, Inc., 1984.

Sodetaini-Shibata. "The Japanese American." In *Culture and Childrearing,* edited by Ann L. Clark. Philadelphia: F. A. Davis Company, 1981, 96–139.

Some, Sobonfu. *The Spirit of Intimacy: Ancient African Teachings in the Ways of Relationships.* New York: HarperCollins/Quill, 2000.

Soto, Lourdes Diaz. *Language, Culture, and Power: Bilingual Families and the Struggle for Quality Education.* New York: State College of New York Press, 1997.

_____. "Understanding Bicultural/Bilingual Young Children." *Young Children 46,* no. 2 (January 1991).

Soto, Lourdes Diaz, and Jocelynn L. Smrekar. "The Politics of Early Bilingual Education." In *Reconceptualizing the Early Childhood Curriculum: Beginning the Dialogue,* edited by Shirley A. Kessler and Beth Blue Swadener. New York: Teachers College Press, 1992, 189–203.

Spencer, Margaret Beale, Geraldine Kearse Brookins, and Allen Walter Recharde, eds. *Beginnings: The Social and Affective Development of Black Children.* Hillsdale, N.J.: Lawrence Erlbaum, 1985.

Stewart, Edward C. *American Cultural Patterns: A Cross-Cultural Perspective.* Yarmouth, Me.: Intercultural Press, 1972.

Stipek, D. "Differences Between Americans and Chinese in the Circumstances Evoking Pride, Shame, and Guilt." *Journal of Cross-Cultural Psychology 29,* no. 5 (1998): 616–629.

Stott, Frances, and Barbara Bowman. "Child Development Knowledge: A Slippery Base for Practice." *Early Childhood Research Quarterly 11,* no. 2 (1996): 1169–1184.

Storti, Craig. *The Art of Crossing Cultures.* Yarmouth, Me.: Intercultural Press, 1990.

Stringfellow, Lorraine, Nguyen Dang Liem, and Linda Liem. "The Vietnamese in America." In *Culture and Childrearing,* edited by Ann Linda Clark. Philadelphia: F. A. Davis Company, 1981.

Sturm, Connie. "Intercultural Communication in Child Care: Creating Parent-Teacher Dialogue." Master's thesis, 1995.

Sue, Stanley, and Thom Moore, eds. *The Pluralistic Society.* New York: Human Sciences Press, Inc., 1984.

Sung, B. L. *Chinese Immigrant Children in New York City: The Experience of Adjustment.* New York: Center for Migration Studies, 1987.

Takaki, Ronald. *A Different Mirror: A History of Multicultural America.* Boston: Back Bay Books, 1993.

Tedla, Elleni. *Sankofa: African Thought and Education.* New York: Peter Lang, 1995.

Tobaissen, Dora Pulido, and Janet Gonzalez-Mena. *A Place to Begin: Working with Parents on Issues of Diversity.* Oakland, Calif.: California Tomorrow, 1998.

Tobin, Joseph J., David Y. H. Wu, and Dana H. Davidson. *Preschool in Three Cultures.* New Haven, Conn.: Yale University Press, 1989.

Trawick-Smith, Jeffrey. *Early Childhood Development: A Multicultural Perspective.* Columbus, Ohio: Merrill, 1997.

Valdes, Guadalupe. *Con Respecto: Bridging the Distances Between Culturally Diverse Families and Schools.* New York: Teachers College Press, 1996.

Villarruel, Francisco A., David R. Imig, and Marjorie J. Kostelnik. "Diverse Families." In *Meeting the Challenge of Linguistic and Cultural Diversity in Early Childhood Education,* edited by Eugene E. Garcia and Barry McLaughlin, with Bernard Spokek and Olivia N. Saracho. New York: Teachers College Press, 1995, 103–124.

Wardel, Francis. "Are You Sensitive to Interracial Children's Special Identity Needs?" *Young Children 42,* no. 2 (January 1987): 53–59.

_____. "Endorsing Children's Differences: Meeting the Needs of Adopted Minority Children." *Young Children 45,* no. 5 (July 1990): 44–46.

Whiting, Beatrice Blyth, and Carolyn Pope Edwards. *Children of Different Worlds: The Formation of Social Behavior.* Cambridge, Mass.: Harvard University Press, 1988.

Williams, Leslie R. "Developmentally Appropriate Practice and Cultural Values: A Case in Point." In *Diversity and Developmentally Appropriate Practices: Challenges for Early Childhood Education,* edited by Bruce L. Mallory and Rebecca S. New. New York: Teachers College Press, 1994, 155–165.

Wong-Fillmore, Lilly. "When Learning a Second Language Means Losing the First." *Early Childhood Research Quarterly 6* (1991): 323–345.

Wright, Marguerite A. *I'm Chocolate, You're Vanilla: Raising Healthy Black and White Children in a Race-Conscious World.* San Francisco: Jossey-Bass, 1998.

Wu, D. "Chinese Childhood Socialization." In *The Handbook of Chinese Psychology,* edited by M. H. Bond. Hong Kong: Oxford University Press, 1996, 143–154.

York, Stacy. *Roots and Wings: Affirming Culture in Early Childhood Programs.* St. Paul, Minn.: Redleaf Press, 1991.

Fiction and Personal Narratives

Alvarez, Julia. *How the Garcia Girls Lost Their Accents.* New York: Penguin Books, 1991.

Angelou, Maya. *I Know Why the Caged Bird Sings.* New York: Bantam, 1969.

Atwood, Margaret. *Cat's Eye. New* York: Doubleday, 1988.

Bogdan, Robert, and Steven J. Biklen. *The Social Meaning of Mental Retardation: Two Life Stories.* New York: Teachers College Press, 1992.

Brown, Claude. *Manchild in the Promised Land.* New York: Macmillan, 1965.

Bryant, Dorothy. *Miss Giardino.* Berkeley: Ata Books, 1978.

Castillo, Ana. *The Mixquiahuala Letters.* New York: Anchor Books, 1986.

_____. *Sapogonia.* New York: Anchor Books, 1991.

_____. *So Far from God.* New York: Penguin Books, 1994.

Cather, Willa. *My Antonia.* New York: Bantam Books, 1994.

Cisneros, Sandra. *The House on Mango Street.* New York: Vintage, 1989.

Crow Dog, Mary. *Lakota Woman.* New York: Weidenfeld, 1990.

Dillard, Annie. *An American Childhood.* New York: Harper and Row, 1987.

Doig, Ivan. *This House of Sky: Landscapes of a Western Mind.* New York: Harcourt Brace Jovanovich, 1978.

Doyle, Roddy. *Paddy Clarke, Ha, Ha, Ha.* London: Secker and Warburg, 1993.

Erdrich, Louise. *Love Medicine.* New York: HarperPerennial, 1984.

Erikson, Erik. *Young Man Luther.* New York: Norton, 1958.

Garcia, Cristina. *Dreaming in Cuban.* New York: Knopf, 1992.

Gibbons, Kaye. *Ellen Fosters.* New York: Vintage Contemporaries, 1987.

Harris, Wilson. *Palace of the Peacock.* London: Faber and Faber, 1960.

hooks, bell. *Sisters of the Yam: Black Women and Self-Recovery.* Boston: South End Press, 1993.

Kincaid, Jamaica. *Annie John.* New York: Penguin Books, 1985.

_____. *Lucy.* New York: Penguin Books, 1990.

Kingston, Maxine Hong. *Woman Warrior.* New York: Vintage International, 1989.

Lamott, Anne. *Operating Instructions.* New York: Fawcett Columbine, 1993.

Maclean, Norman. *A River Runs Through It.* New York: Pocket Books, 1976.

Martinez, Demetria. *Mother Tongue.* Tempe, Arizona: Bilingual Press, 1994.

Morrison, Toni. *The Bluest Eye.* New York: Pocket Books, 1970.

_____. *Beloved.* New York: Pocket Books, 1987.

Mukherjee, Bharati. *Jasmine.* New York: Ballantine Books, 1989.

Olsen, Tillie. *Tell Me a Riddle.* New York: Delacorte Press/Seymour Lawrence, 1961.

Pilcher, Rosamunde. *September.* New York: St. Martin's Press, 1990.

Qoyawayma, Poligaysi. *No Turning Back.* Albuquerque: University of New Mexico Press, 1964.

Sears, James T. *Growing Up Gay in the South: Race, Gender, and Journeys of the Spirit.* New York: The Haworth Press, 1991.

Silko, Leslie Marmon. *Ceremony.* New York: Viking, 1977.

_____. *Storyteller.* New York: Seaver, 1981.

X, Malcolm, with Alex Haley. *The Autobiography of Malcolm X.* New York: Ballantine Books, 1964.

Videos

California Department of Education

Coproduced with the Far West Laboratory/WestEd. Videos are available in English, Spanish, and Chinese (Cantonese).

Child Development Division, 560 J Street, Suite 220, Sacramento, CA 95814, (800) 995-4099

Program for Infant/Toddler Caregivers Training Series

The Ages of Infancy (26 min.)	Caring for young, mobile, and older infants.
Discoveries of Infancy (32 min.)	Cognitive development and learning.
Early Messages (29 min.)	Communicating with Infants and Toddlers
Essential Connections (36 min.)	Ten keys to culturally sensitive child care.
First Moves (27 min.)	Welcoming a child to a new caregiving setting.
Flexible, Fearful, or Feisty (29 min.)	The different temperaments of infants and toddlers.
Getting in Tune (24 min.)	Creating nurturing relationships with infants and toddlers.
Ingredients for a Good Start (25 min.)	How to provide healthy foods for young children.
In Our Hands (12 min.)	The importance of quality care for infants and toddlers.
It's Not Just Routine (24 min.)	Feeding, diapering, and napping/infants and toddlers.
Protective Urges (30 min.)	Parent/provider relationships.
Respectfully Yours (58 min.)	Magda Gerber's approach to professional infant/toddler care.
Room at the Table (23 min.)	Meeting Children's Special Needs at Mealtime
Space to Grow (22 min.)	Creating a child-care environment for infants and toddlers.
Together in Care (30 min.)	Meeting the intimacy needs of infants and toddlers in groups.

Childhood

A production of WNET and The Childhood Project, Inc., in association with Channel 4 Television (Great Britain).

Ambrose Video Publishing, Inc., 28 West 44th Street, Suite 2100, New York, NY 10036, (800) 526-4663, http://www.AmbroseVideo.com/

Among Equals (60 min.)	Cultural variation in middle childhood experiences, gender roles and sex differences, and moral development.

Great Expectations (60 min.)	The theme of the influence of nature and nurture plays out in five families throughout the world.
In the Land of Giants (60 min.)	Birth order, sibling rivalry, and independence through dependence.
Life's Lessons (60 min.)	Biosocial development of school-age children, the "five-to-seven shift," and cultural variation in education.
Louder Than Words (60 min.)	Development in the first months of life and cultural aspects of caregiving.
Love's Labors (60 min.)	The milestones of early childhood, including moral development and a sense of self, and child-care issues.

DC/TATS Media

Frank Porter Graham Child Development Center, University of North Carolina, Chapel Hill, 105 Smith Level Road, Chapel Hill, NC 27599, (919) 966-2622, http://www.fpg.unc.edu/

Building Self-Confidence (30 min.)	Looks at how caregivers and parents can develop self-confidence and a positive self concept in young children.
Establishing Healthful Habits (30 min.)	Suggests habits that promote wellness, as well as solutions to health threats in daycare settings.
Harmonizing the Worlds of Home and Child Care (30 min.)	Explores ways to reduce family stress through cooperation.
Listening and Talking (30 min.)	Explains how language develops as a medium for communication and thinking.
Meeting Special Needs (30 min.)	Based on the work of Thelma Harms and Debby Cryer, this program focuses on parents' alternatives for the care and education of young children with special needs.
The Nurturing Community (30 min.)	Thelma Harms and Debby Cryer explore child-rearing choices and the reasons parents make certain choices.
Playing and Learning (30 min.)	Explains the stages of preschool play as the way to learn from infancy through kindergarten.
Relating to Others (30 min.)	Looks at positive ways adults can help children develop skills such as empathy and sharing.
A Secure Beginning (30 min.)	Follows the development of children's relationships to others.
Thinking and Creativity (30 min.)	Thelma Harms and Debby Cryer explore thinking.

Herzog Media

Herzog Associates, 2511 Mt. Beacon Terrace, Los Angeles, CA 90068, (323)466-7091, www.herzog-media.com

Diversity

Reconciling Contradictions: Equitable Solutions to Cultural Differences (29 minutes)

Manitoba Child Care Association
364 McGregor St., Winnipeg, MB R2W 4X3, (204) 586-8587

Series of 6 videos each 15–18 minutes

Our Children, Our Ways: Early Childhood Education in First Nations and Inuit Communities
Child Care in Our Communities
Speaking Our Languages
Exploring the Natural World
Music and Dance
Telling Stories, Reading Books
Supporting Children's Art

Magna Systems

95 West County Line Road, Barrington, IL 60010, (800) 203-7060, http://www.webering.com/magna/
Each video is approximately 30 minutes in length.

Early Childhood Training Series

Diversity
Diversity and Communication
Diversity and Conflict Management
Diversity: Contrasting Perspectives
Diversity, Independence, and Individuality
Diversity: Reconciling Contradictions
Path to Math
Number and Counting: Numerals
One to One Correspondence: Comparing
Sets and Classification: Seriation (Ordering)
Shape: Parts and Wholes
Space: Measurement

The Developing Child Series

Study of the Child
History and Trends
Observation
Theories of Development
Beginnings of Life
Heredity and the Environment: Blueprints for a Baby
The Newborn: Development and Discovery
Prenatal Development: A Life in the Making
Pregnancy and Birth: Caring and Preparing for the Life Within
Infancy
Infancy: Beginnings in Cognition and Language
Infancy: Early Relationships
Infancy: Landmarks of Development
Infancy: Self and Social World
Meeting the Needs of Children
The Child in the Family
Early Child Care and Education
Exceptional Children
Nutrition

Toddlerhood/Preschoolers
 Preschoolers: Physical and Cognitive Development
 Preschoolers: Social and Emotional Development
 Toddlerhood: Emotional Development
 Toddlerhood: Physical and Cognitive Development
Significant Areas of Development
 Play
 Language Development
 Moral Development
 Self-Identity and Sex Role Development
Middle Childhood
 Middle Childhood: Cognitive and Language Development
 Middle Childhood: Physical Growth and Development
 Middle Childhood: Social and Emotional Development

National Association for the Education of Young Children (NAEYC)

1509 16th Street N.W._Washington, D.C. 20036-1426_(800) 424-2460_http://www.naeyc.org/

The Adventure Begins: Preschool and Technology (10 min.)
Appropriate Curriculum for Young Children: The Role of the Teacher (28 min.)
Before and After School . . . Creative Experiences (28 min.)
Block Play: Constructing Realities (20 min.)
Building Quality Child Care: An Overview (20 min.)
Building Quality Child Care: Independence (20 min.)
Building Quality Child Care Relationships (15 min.)
Career Encounters: Early Childhood Education (28 min.)
Caring for Infants and Toddlers (17 min.)
Caring for Our Children Series (six 30-minute tapes)
Celebrating Early Childhood Teachers (22 min.)
Charting Growth—Assessment (30 min.)
Child Care Administration: Tying It All Together (28 min.)
A Classroom with Blocks (13 min.)
Culture and Education of Young Children (16 min.)
Curriculum for Preschool and Kindergarten (16 min.)
Designing Developmentally Appropriate Days (28 min.)
Developmentally Appropriate First Grade: A Community of Learners (30 min.)
Developmentally Appropriate Practice: Birth Through Age 5 (27 min.)
Discipline: Appropriate Guidance of Young Children (28 min.)
Doing a Self-Study: Why and How? (30 min.)
Early Intervention: Natural Environments for Children (28 min.)
Environments for Young Children (18 min.)
Exploring Science and Nature (28 min.)
Food for Thought: Nutrition and Children (28 min.)
The Full Cost of Quality in Early Childhood Programs (25 min.)
How Young Children Learn to Think (19 min.)
An Idea Blossoms—Integrated Curriculum (30 min.)

Infant Curriculum: Great Explorations (20 min.)
Make a Difference: Report Child Abuse and Neglect (28 min.)
Men Caring for Young Children (30 min.)
Mister Rogers Talks with Parents (43 min.)
Music Across the Curriculum (20 min.)
Nurturing Growth—Child Growth and Development (30 min.)
Painting a Positive Picture: Proactive Behavior Management (28 min.)
Partnerships with Parents (28 min.)
Places to Grow—The Learning Environment (30 min.)
Play and Learning (18 min.)
Play—The Seed of Learning (30 min.)
Quality Family Child Care (28 min.)
Reading and Young Children (15 min.)
Reason to Care: Corporate Support of Community Child Care (28 min.)
Relating to Others (17 min.)
Safe Active Play: A Guide to Avoiding Play Area Hazards
Salaries, Working Conditions, and the Teacher Shortage (17 min.)
Seeds of Change—Leadership and Staff Development (30 min.)
Seeing Infants with New Eyes (26 min.)
Sensory Play: Constructing Realities (18 min.)
Sharing Nature with Young Children (18 min.)
Structured Play: Gross Motor Activities for Every Day (28 min.)
Teachers in Transition: Room to Grow (23 min.)
Teaching the Whole Child in the Kindergarten (27 min.)
Toddler Curriculum: Making Connections (20 min.)
Using the Early Childhood Classroom Observation (26 min.)
What Is Quality Child Care? (53 min.)
Whole-Language Learning (20 min.)
Windows on Learning: A Framework for Making Decisions (20 min.)

Redleaf Press

450 N. Syndicate, Suite 5, St. Paul, MN 55104-4125, (800) 423-8309

Anti-Bias Curriculum (30 min.)	Direct care staff discuss why the Anti-Bias Curriculum is important to them and how they implement it. User's guide included.
We All Belong (20 min.)	Learn the principles that transformed this Australian center into a place where everyone feels at home. Ideal for program planning. User's guide included.

Ryerson's School of Early Childhood Education

Ryerson Polytechnic University, 350 Victoria St., Toronto, Ont., Canada M5B 2K3, (416) 979-5000

Multi-Age in Action (21 min.)	Exploring the inclusion of multi-age groups in group, licensed child care and education.

ECE on the Internet

ECE Net

http://ericps.ed.uiuc.edu/eece/listserv/ecenet-1.html

The ECE net is a national information system. The address to subscribe to the ECE net is listserv@postoffice.cso.uiuc.edu. Subscriptions are free of charge. To sign up use the above address and write on the subject line SUBSCRIBEECENET-L followed by your full name. Subscribers include teachers and students of early childhood education and care programs, including those that focus primarily on infants, toddlers, preschool, kindergarten, and primary. The topics on this listserv vary widely, as subscribers bring their questions, concerns, and issues to their fellow early childhood educators.

ERIC

http://ericps.ed.uiuc.edu/

ERIC is the clearinghouse on Elementary and Early Childhood Education at the University of Illinois, Urbana-Champaign. It is a listserv supported by the U.S. Department of Education and includes listings of publications, including books, digests, resource lists, and the ERIC/EECE Newsletter. AskERIC and Parents AskERIC is an Internet-based question-answering service sponsored by the ERIC system. ERIC also has listserv discussion groups on topics related to early childhood education and beyond. One such discussion group deals with topics related to Reggio Emilia, the early childhood education system of the city of Reggio in northern Italy. Subscribers ask one another questions, as well as describe their challenges and triumphs as they try to implement a Reggio-inspired approach in their various programs.

National Association for the Education of Young Children (NAEYC)

http://www.america-tomorrow.com/naeyc

NAEYC offers services to adults who work with children, such as a peer-reviewed journal, books and videos, conferences, and opportunities for public advocacy. The Web site also offers links to affiliate groups.

National Child Care Information Center

http://ericps.ed.uiuc.edu/nccic/nccichome.html

The NCCIC is an adjunct ERIC clearinghouse for child care under the U.S. Department of Health and Human Services; Administration for Children and Families; Administration on Children, Youth, and Families; and Child Care Bureau. The Child Care Bureau, which sponsors the NCCIC, was established in January 1995 to improve quality, availability, and affordability of child care as well as to administer federal child-care programs to states, territories, and tribes for low-income children and families. NCCIC publishes the Child Care Bulletin and provides tribal resources, a conference calendar, and current information on welfare reform, among other services.

U.S. Department of Education

http://www.ed.gov/index.html

This Web site includes information on legislation, funding opportunities, statistical data, and tips on accessing other Internet resources.

Additional Web sites

About the Care and Education of Infants and Toddlers

www.ehsnrc.org	Database of all the Early Head Start program sites as well as valuable tips and strategies for trainers and many full-text documents on a range of infant/toddler related topics.
www.infanttoddlerconsortium.org	California organization dedicated to improving infant-toddler care.
www.pitc.org	Program for Infant-Toddler Caregivers supports and promotes quality care for infants and toddlers through resources, information, and training.
www.rie.org	Resources for Infant Educarers is a nonprofit organization that, using the teachings of Magda Gerber, has developed and is teaching a unique philosophy and methodology in working with infants.
www.zerotothree.org	Zero to Three: National Center for Infants, Toddlers, and Families, for parents and professionals. The nation's leading resource on the first three years of life whose mission is to strengthen and support families, practitioners and communities to promote the healthy development of babies and toddlers. Some information in Spanish.

Health and Safety in Early Childhood Programs

http://www.aap.org/	American Academy of Pediatrics (AAP).
www.childcarehealth.org	The Child Care Healthline provides answers to a variety of questions concerning health, safety, nutrition, caring for children with special needs, child abuse, and violence prevention.
http://vm.cfsan.fda.gov/list.html	For food safety information.
http://www.cdc.gov/	Centers for Disease Control. Surveillance for food-borne disease outbreaks.
http://www.nal.usda.gov/fnic/foodborne/foodborn.htm	USDA/FDA Food-borne Illness Education Center gives links to other food safety sites, food safety.

http://www.epa.gov/ | U.S. Environmental Protection Agency gives information about pesticides and water quality.

Project Work in Early Childhood Programs

http://www.project-approach.com | Information and resources related to using what is called a "project-approach" curriculum for engaging children's minds.

Diversity and Early Childhood Education

www.californiatomorrow.org | Research and training in diversity issues of language, culture, and race related to early childhood education.

www.childrensdefense.org | The mission of the Children's Defense Fund is to ensure every child a good and moral start in life with the help of caring families and communities. Anti-bias resources.

http://clas.uiuc.edu/ | Web page of the Culturally and Linguistically Appropriate Services Early Childhood Research Institute, which specializes in resources for those working with children who have special needs.

www.herzogmedia.com | Videos and information about diversity.

Special Education/Inclusion in Early Childhood Programs

esr@wested.org | Information and resource materials for early intervention for infants and toddlers with special needs.

www.circleofinclusion.org | Information for early childhood service providers and families of young children including information about the effective practices of inclusive educational programs for children from birth through age eight.

www.familyvillage.wisc.edu | Disability-related resources that include informational resources on specific diagnoses, communication connections, adaptive products, and more.

www.nichcy.org | National information and referral center that provides information on disabilities and disability-related issues for families, educators, and other professionals. The focus is birth to age 22.

www.npnd.org | National Parent Network on Disabilities (NPND) has as its mission to provide a presence and national voice for families of children, youth, and adults with disabilities.

www.thearc.org | The Arc of the United States is the national organization of and for people with mental retardation and related disabilities and their families.

www.cec.sped.org

The Council for Exceptional Children is dedicated to improving educational outcomes for individuals with exceptionalities. CEC advocates for appropriate governmental policies, sets professional standards, provides continual professional development, and helps professionals obtain conditions and resources necessary for effective professional practice.

www.irsc.org

Internet Resources for Special Children (IRSC) Web site is dedicated to communicating information relating to the needs of children with disabilities to parents and professionals.

Miscellaneous Information About Early Childhood Education/Child Care

www.naccrra.net

National Association of Child Care Resource and Referral Agencies (NACCRRA) is a national network of community-based child care resource and referral agencies and provides a common ground where families, child care providers, and communities can share information about quality child care.

www.ccw.org

Center for Child Care Workforce advocates for increased status and wages for early childhood professionals.

www.providerappreciation.org

Provider Appreciation Day is a nonprofit corporation to promote meaningful ways for parents and organizations to express their appreciation to child care providers.

www.stand.org

Stand for Children is a campaign to increase national and local awareness of the needs of children.

NAEYC Standards
and Position Papers

NAEYC Early Childhood Program Standards

Focus Area: Children

Program Standard 1: Relationships

The program promotes positive relationships among all children and adults to encourage each child's sense of individual worth and belonging as part of a community, and to foster each child's ability to contribute as a responsible community member.

Rationale: Positive relationships are essential for the development of personal responsibility, capacity for self-regulation, and for constructive interactions with others. Warm, sensitive, and responsive interactions help children develop a secure, positive sense of self and encourage them to respect and cooperate with others. Children who see themselves as highly valued are more likely to feel secure, thrive physically, get along with others, learn well, and feel part of a community.

Program Standard 2: Curriculum

The program implements a curriculum that is consistent with its goals for children and promotes learning and development in each of the following domains: aesthetic, cognitive, emotional, language, physical, and social.

Rationale: Curriculum that is goal-oriented and incorporates concepts and skills based on current research fosters children's learning and development. When informed by teachers' knowledge of individual children, a well-articulated curriculum guides teachers so they can provide children with experiences that foster growth across a broad range of developmental and content areas. It also brings intentionality to planning a daily schedule that incorporates time and materials for play, self-initiated learning, and creative expression, and provides opportunities for children to learn individually and in groups according to their developmental needs and interests.

Program Standard 3: Teaching

The program uses developmentally, culturally, and linguistically appropriate and effective teaching approaches that enhance each child's learning and development in the context of the program's curriculum goals.

Rationale: Teachers who use multiple instructional approaches optimize children's opportunities for learning. These approaches include strategies that range from structured to unstructured and adult-directed to child-directed. Children bring different backgrounds, interests, experiences, learning styles, needs, and capacities to learning environments. Teachers' consideration of these differences when selecting and implementing instructional approaches helps all children to succeed. Instructional approaches also differ in their effectiveness for teaching different elements of curriculum and learning. For a program to address the complexity inherent in any teaching-learning situation, a variety of effective instructional approaches must be employed.

Program Standard 4: Assessment

The program is informed by ongoing systematic, formal, and informal assessment approaches to provide information on children's learning and development. These assessments occur within the context of reciprocal communications with families and with sensitivity to the cultural contexts in which children develop. Assessment results are used to benefit children by informing sound decisions about children, teaching, and program improvement.

Rationale: Teachers' knowledge of each child helps them to plan appropriately challenging curriculum and to tailor instruction that responds to each child's strengths and needs. Further, systematic assessment is essential for identifying children who may benefit from more intensive instruction or intervention or who may need additional developmental evaluation. This information ensures that the program meets its goals for children's learning and developmental progress and also informs program improvement efforts.

Program Standard 5: Health

The program promotes the nutrition and health of all children and staff and protects them from preventable illness and injury.

Rationale: To benefit from education and maintain quality of life, children need to be as healthy as possible. Children depend on adults, who also are as healthy as possible, to make healthful choices for them and to teach them to make such choices for themselves. While some degree of risk taking is desirable for learning, a high quality program prevents hazardous practices and environments likely to result in adverse consequences for children, staff, families or communities.

Focus Area: Teaching Staff

Program Standard 6: Teachers

The program employs and supports a teaching staff that has the educational qualifications, knowledge, and professional commitment necessary to promote children's learning and development and to support families' diverse needs and interests.

Rationale: Children benefit most when their teachers have high levels of formal education and specialized early childhood professional preparation. Teachers who have specific preparation, knowledge and skills in child development and early childhood education are more likely to engage in warm, positive interactions with children, offer richer language experiences, and create more high-quality learning environments. Opportunities for teaching staff to receive supportive supervision and to participate in ongoing professional development ensure that their knowledge and skills reflect the profession's ever-changing knowledge base.

Focus Area: Family and Community Partnerships

Program Standard 7: Families

The program establishes and maintains collaborative relationships with each child's family to foster children's development in all settings. These relationships are sensitive to family composition, language, and culture.

Rationale: Young children's learning and development are integrally connected to their families. Consequently, to support and promote children's optimal learning and development, programs need to recognize the primacy of children's families; establish relationships with families based on mutual trust and respect; support and involve families in their children's educational growth; and invite families to fully participate in the program.

Program Standard 8: Communities

The program establishes relationships with and uses the resources of the children's communities to support the achievement of program goals.

Rationale: As part of the fabric of children's communities, an effective program establishes and maintains reciprocal relationships with agencies and institutions that can support it in achieving its goals for curriculum, health promotion, children's transitions, inclusion, and diversity. By helping to connect families with needed resources, the program furthers children's healthy development and learning.

Focus Area: Leadership and Administration

Program Standard 9: Physical Environment

The program provides appropriate and well-maintained indoor and outdoor physical environments, including facilities, equipment, and materials, to facilitate child and staff learning and development. To this end, a program structures a safe and healthful environment.

Rationale: The program's design and maintenance of its physical environment support high-quality program activities and services and allow for optimal use and operation. Well-organized, equipped, and maintained environments support program quality by facilitating the learning, comfort, health, and safety of those who use the program. By also creating a welcoming and accessible setting for children, families, and staff, program quality is enhanced.

Program Standard 10: Leadership and Management

The program effectively implements policies, procedures, and systems in support of stable staff and strong personnel, fiscal, and program management so that all children, families and staff have high-quality experiences.

Rationale: Excellent programming requires effective governance structures, competent and knowledgeable leadership, and comprehensive and well functioning administrative policies, procedures, and systems. Effective leadership and administration create the environment for high-quality care and education by: assuring compliance with relevant regulations and guidelines; promoting fiscal soundness, program accountability, effective communication, helpful consultative services, positive community relations, and provision of a comfortable and supportive workplace; maintaining stable staff; and instituting opportunities for ongoing program planning for staff and career development and for continuous program improvement.

Go to www.naeyc.org to read the full statement.

National Association for the Education of Young Children

Position Paper: Responding to Linguistic and Cultural Diversity

Recommendations for Effective Early Childhood Education

Linguistically and culturally diverse is an educational term used by the U.S. Department of Education to define children enrolled in educational programs who are either non-English- proficient (NEP) or limited-English-proficient(LEP). Educators use this phrase, linguistically and culturally diverse, to identify children from homes and communities where English is not the primary language of communication. For the purposes of this statement, the phrase will be used in a similar manner.

This document primarily describes linguistically and culturally diverse children who speak languages other than English. However, the recommendations of this position statement can also apply to children who, although they speak only English, are also linguistically and culturally diverse.

The children and families served in early childhood programs reflect the ethnic, cultural, and linguistic diversity of the nation. The nation's children all deserve an early childhood education that is responsive to their families, communities, and racial, ethnic, and cultural backgrounds. For young children to develop and learn optimally, the early childhood professional must be prepared to meet their diverse developmental, cultural, linguistic, and educational needs. Early childhood educators face the challenge of how best to respond to these needs.

The acquisition of language is essential to children's cognitive and social development. Regardless of what language children speak, they still develop and learn. Educators recognize that linguistically and culturally diverse children come to early childhood programs with previously acquired knowledge and learning based upon the language used in their home. For young children, the language of the home is the language they have used since birth, the language they use to make and establish meaningful communicative relationships, and the language they use to begin to construct their knowledge and test their learning. The home language is tied to children's culture, and culture and language communicate traditions, values, and attitudes. Parents should be encouraged to use and develop children's home language; early childhood educators should respect children's linguistic learning styles. In so doing, adults will enhance children's learning and development.

NAEYC's goal is to build support for equal access to high-quality educational programs that recognize and promote all aspects of children's development and learning, enabling all children to become competent, successful, and socially responsible adults. Children's educational experiences should afford them the opportunity to learn and to become effective, functioning members of society. Language development is essential for learning, and the development of children's home language does not interfere with their ability to learn English. Because knowing more than one language is a cognitive asset, early education programs should encourage the development of children's home language while fostering the acquisition of English.

For the optimal development and learning of all children, educators must **accept** the legitimacy of children's home language, **respect** (hold in high regard) and **value** (esteem, appreciate), the home culture, and **promote** and **encourage** the active involvement and support of all families, including extended and nontraditional family units.

When early childhood educators acknowledge and respect children's home language and culture, ties between the family and programs are strengthened. This atmosphere provides increased opportunity for learning because young children feel supported, nurtured, and connected not only to their home communities and families but also to teachers and the educational setting.

The full text of this position statement includes recommendations for a responsive learning environment with a) recommendations for working with children; b) recommendations for working with families; c) recommendations for professional preparation of early childhood educators; and d) recommendations for programs and practice.

NAEYC Position Statement Summary, Adopted November 1995
National Association for the Education of Young Children

Overview of Learning to Read and Write: Developmentally Appropriate Practices for Young Children

A joint position of the International Reading Association (IRA) and the National Association for the Education of Young Children (NAEYC)

> *This joint NAEYC/IRA position statement is endorsed by the following organizations: American Speech-Language-Hearing Association, Association for Childhood Education International, Association of Teacher Educators, Council for Early Childhood Professional Recognition, Division for Early Childhood/Council for Exceptional Children, National Association of Early Childhood Specialists in State Departments of Education, National Association of Early Childhood Teacher Educators, National Association of Elementary School Principals, National Association of State Directors of Special Education, National Council of Teachers of English, Zero to Three/National Center for Infants, Toddlers, & Families.*
>
> *The concepts in this joint position statement are supported by the following organizations: American Academy of Pediatrics, American Association of School Administrators, American Educational Research Association, and the National Head Start Association.*

Learning to read and write is critical to a child's success in school and later in life. One of the best predictors of whether a child will function competently in school and go on to contribute actively in our increasingly literate society is the level to which the child progresses in reading and writing. Although reading and writing abilities continue to develop throughout the life span, the early childhood years—from birth through age eight—are the most important period for literacy development. It is for this reason that the International Reading Association (IRA) and the National Association for the Education of Young Children (NAEYC) joined together to formulate a position statement regarding early literacy development. The statement consists of a set of principles and recommendations for teaching practices and public policy.

The primary purpose of this position statement is to provide guidance to teachers of young children in schools and early childhood programs (including child care centers, preschools, and family child care homes) serving children from birth through age eight. By and large, the principles and practices suggested here also will be of interest to any adults who are in a position to influence a young child's learning and development—parents, grandparents, older siblings, tutors, and other community members.

Teachers work in schools or programs regulated by administrative policies as well as available resources. Therefore secondary audiences for this position statement are school principals and program administrators whose roles are critical in establishing a supportive climate for sound, developmentally appropriate teaching practices; and policymakers whose decisions determine whether adequate resources are available for high-quality early childhood education.

A great deal is known about how young children learn to read and write and how they can be helped toward literacy during the first five years of life. A great deal is known also about how to help children once compulsory schooling begins, whether in kindergarten or the primary grades. Based on a thorough review of the research, this document reflects the commitment of two major professional organizations to the goal of helping children learn to read well enough by the end of third grade so that they can read to learn in all curriculum areas. IRA and NAEYC are committed not only to helping young children learn to read and write but also to fostering and sustaining their interest and disposition to read and write for their own enjoyment, information, and communication.

First, the statement summarizes the current issues that are the impetus for this position; then it reviews what is known from research on young children's literacy development. This review of research as well as the collective wisdom and experience of IRA and NAEYC members provides the basis for a position statement about what constitutes developmentally appropriate practice in early literacy over the period of birth through age eight. The position concludes with recommendations for teaching practices and policies.

To read the full text of the position statement, go to: www.naeyc.org/resources/position statement/psread0.htm

IRA & NAEYC Position Statement, Adopted May 1998
National Association for the Education of Young Children

Position Statement: Early Childhood Mathematics: Promoting Good Beginnings

A joint position of the National Association for the Education of Young Children (NAEYC) and the National Council of Teachers of Mathematics (NCTM)

Position

The National Council of Teachers of Mathematics and the National Association for the Education of Young Children affirm that high-quality, challenging, and accessible mathematics education for three-to-six-year-old children is a vital foundation for future mathematics learning. In every early childhood setting, children should experience effective, research-based curriculum and teaching practices. Such high-quality practice in turn requires policies, organizational supports, and adequate resources that enable teachers to do this challenging and important work.

Rationale

As a society, we are becoming more aware of the importance of early experience in learning to read and write. A similar awareness with respect to mathematics is critical. Early childhood mathematics has a growing knowledge base about learning and teaching as well as an expanding array of research-based curriculum resources. Teachers are eager to provide young children with good beginnings. Now professional preparation programs, education agencies, policymakers, and other partners must mobilize the commitment and resources to apply what we know, support teachers' work, and generate significant progress in early childhood mathematics.

Recommendations

In high-quality mathematics education for three-to-six-year-old children, teachers and other key professionals should

- enhance children's natural interest in mathematics and their disposition to use it to make sense of their physical and social worlds;
- build on children's varying experiences, including their family, linguistic, and cultural backgrounds; their individual approaches to learning; and their informal knowledge;
- base mathematics curriculum and teaching practices on current knowledge of young children's cognitive, linguistic, physical, and social-emotional development;
- use curriculum and teaching practices that strengthen children's problem-solving and reasoning processes as well as representing, communicating, and connecting mathematical ideas;
- ensure that the curriculum is coherent and compatible with known relationships and sequences of important mathematical ideas;
- provide for children's deep and sustained interaction with key mathematical ideas;
- integrate mathematics with other activities and other activities with mathematics;
- provide ample time, materials, and teacher support for children to engage in play, a context in which they explore and manipulate mathematical ideas with keen interest;
- actively introduce mathematical concepts, methods, and language through a range of appropriate experiences and teaching strategies;
- support children's learning by thoughtfully and continually assessing all children's mathematical knowledge, skills, and strategies.

To support high-quality mathematics education, institutions, program developers, and policymakers should

- create more effective early childhood teacher preparation and continuing professional development in mathematics;
- use collaborative processes to develop well-aligned systems of appropriate, high-quality standards, mathematics curriculum, and assessment;
- design institutional structures and policies that support teachers' mathematics learning, teamwork, and planning;
- provide resources necessary to overcome the barriers to young children's mathematical proficiency at the classroom, community, institutional, and system-wide levels.

This position is elaborated in the full version of the joint statement at http://www.naeyc.org/resources/position_statements/positions_intro.asp.

National Association for the Education of Young Children

Position on Inclusion

Division for Early Childhood (DEC) of the Council for Exceptional Children

Inclusion, as a value, supports the right of all children, regardless of their diverse abilities, to participate actively in natural settings within their communities. A natural setting is one in which the child would spend time had he or she not had a disability. Such settings include, but are not limited to, home and family, play groups, child care, nursery schools, Head Start programs, kindergartens, and neighborhood school classrooms.

DEC believes in and supports full and successful access to health, social service, education, and other supports and services for young children and their families that promote full participation in community life. DEC values the diversity of families and supports a family-guided process for determining services that are based on the needs and preferences of individual families and children.

To implement inclusive practices, DEC supports (a) the continued development, evaluation, and dissemination of full inclusion supports, services, and systems so that the options for inclusion are of high quality; (b) the development of preservice and inservice training programs that prepare families, administrators, and service providers to develop and work within inclusive settings; (c) collaboration among all key stakeholders to implement flexible fiscal and administrative procedures in support of inclusion; (d) research that contributes to our knowledge of state-of-the-art services; and (e) the restructuring and unification of social, education, health, and intervention supports and services to make them more responsive to the needs of all children and families.

NAEYC Position Statement, Adopted April 1993
(Endorsed by NAEYC November 1993)
National Association for the Education of Young Children